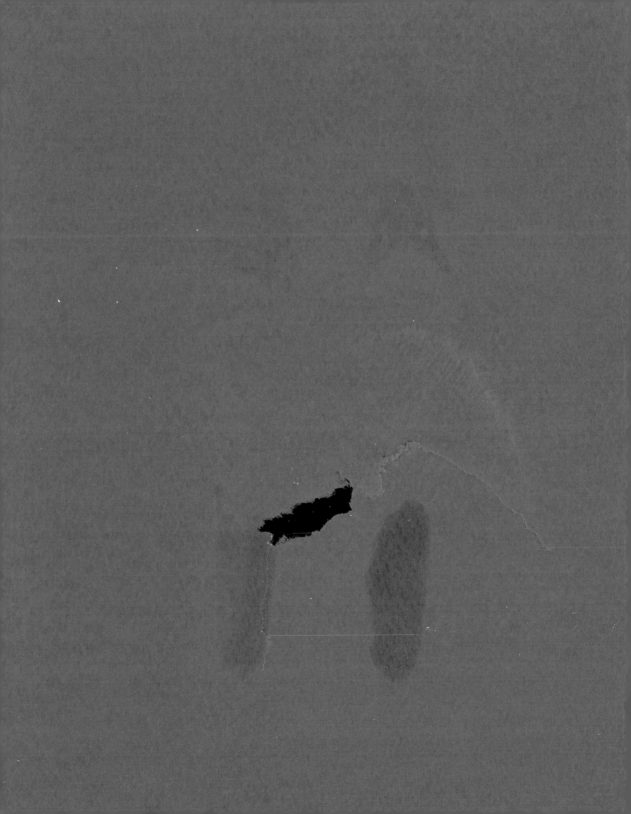

ALTERNATE
ENERGY SOURCES

ALTERNATE ENERGY SOURCES

BY JANE WERNER WATSON

A FIRST BOOK
FRANKLIN WATTS | NEW YORK | LONDON | 1979

FRONTIS: AN ARTIST'S CONCEPTION OF SOLAR ENERGY
BEING CAPTURED AND CONVERTED TO
ELECTRICITY BY A HELIOSTAT-CENTRAL RECEIVER SYSTEM.

Photographs courtesy of United Press International:
frontispiece, pp. 6, 13, 16, 26, 31, and 40 (bottom);
U.S. Department of Energy: pp. 9 (top and bottom),
14, 35, 36 (bottom), and 52 (bottom); NASA: p. 10;
Sandia Laboratories: pp. 17 and 36 (top); Cater-
pillar Tractor Co.: p. 24; Waste Management, Inc.:
p. 28; U.S. Department of Agriculture: p. 32; General Electric for the U.S. Department of Energy:
p. 40 (top); U.S. Bureau of Reclamation: p. 44;
Lockheed Missiles and Space Co., Inc.: p. 47;
Lawrence Berkeley Laboratory: p. 52 (top).

Library of Congress Cataloging in Publication Data

Watson, Jane Werner, 1915–
Alternate energy sources.

(A First book)
Includes index.
SUMMARY: Discusses alternate sources of energy
such as the sun, wind, and water, which are both
renewable and harmless to the environment.
1. Renewable energy sources—Juvenile literature.
[1. Renewable energy sources. 2. Power re-
sources. 3. Energy conservation] I. Title.
TJ163.23.N37   333.7   78–10872
ISBN 0–531–02252–8

CONTENTS

ALTERNATE ENERGY SOURCES

CHAPTER ONE
NATURE'S ENERGY BANK

Scarcely a week passes without **energy** being front-page news. Often the headlines are gloomy:

"NEW YORK DARKENED BY POWER FAILURE."
"ENERGY EMERGENCY DECLARED IN TWO STATES."
"WINTER POWER SHORTAGE THREATENS NORTHEAST."

Other headlines are more hopeful. They tell of experimental work being done in the development of new—**alternate—energy sources** to prevent shortages:

"RADIO STATION POWERED BY WIND."
"ELECTRIC CARS PLUG INTO FUTURE."
"CEREAL CROP PRODUCES POWER."
"NEW FUEL SOURCE FROM WASTES IS SQUARED AWAY."

Headlines like these give us hope for the future, when additional energy sources will be needed even more than they are today.

News, good or bad, about energy is important to everyone, for everything we do and everything that is done for us takes energy. Cars and trucks, airplanes and trains need energy to move. Machines in factories and the lights in office buildings require energy to operate. To cook a meal takes energy. People and animals use energy just moving about. They use more as they work and play.

Shortages of **fuel** and power—of energy—can have dreadful effects. They can leave homes without heat in winter. They can cause factories to close, putting people out of work. Energy shortages can even keep food from being produced and shipped to where it is needed.

To produce energy anywhere on earth takes fuel. The fuels most used today are coal, natural gas, and oil. In 1977, for example, oil supplied 47 percent of the energy used in the United States, natural gas 27 percent, and coal 19 percent. One or another of these fuels is burned to provide heat for buildings, to keep the machines in factories running, and to keep transportation moving.

These same fuels are also burned in power plants to produce **electricity**. There, water heated by the burning fuel turns to steam, and the force of the expanding steam powers **generators**, special machines that convert **mechanical energy** into **electrical energy**. Electricity, in turn, can provide light, heat, or the power needed to run other machines.

All these fuels—coal, oil, and natural gas—are working quite well today. It is true that burning them does pollute the air. And mining and drilling operations do deface the landscape. But the greatest problem related to the use of these fuels is that they are all **fossil fuels**. As such, once used, they cannot be replaced.

Fossils, as you may know, are the remains of long-dead plants or animals, found in rocks. Over the ages the remains of those dead plants or animals were crushed slowly, slowly into rock. In the process of crushing, great heat was created, and layers of coal, pools of oil, and pockets of gas were formed deep underground or in swamps close to the surface.

It would take many hundreds of thousands of years to

replace the earth's store of fossil fuels. Yet within another fifty years, we may have used up nearly all the oil and gas that is within reach of our equipment. Coal reserves will last for some generations longer. But even they will not last forever.

In addition to their being used for heat, light, and power, coal and oil are also used in producing many useful products. These include paints, dyes, plastics, petroleum jellies and greases, and artificial proteins for feeding livestock. We must, therefore, cut down on our use of fossil fuels in time to leave us some stock for the making of these products.

During the past thirty years the element uranium has been hailed as a great alternative energy source. This is because the atoms making up one kind of uranium, U_{235} (so-called because each atom has 235 particles in its nucleus), can be split by a process called **fission**. Fission releases a surprisingly large amount of energy in the form of heat. This **nuclear energy**, as it is generally known, is produced in power plants, and the heat released as the atoms are split is used to turn water to steam. The steam is then used to run steam engines.

Nuclear power plants use very small amounts of U_{235} for fuel. This saves the costly shipping and the using up of large amounts of coal or oil. But there are serious problems related to the use of nuclear energy. For one thing, in the splitting of the atoms, deadly radioactive rays are released. This "radiation," which can be very harmful to human and other life, continues to be given off by the spent fuel for many thousands of years. How to dispose of the used fuel safely has become a real problem.

Some nuclear wastes have been sealed in containers and dumped into the ocean. Later it was found that these containers were leaking, thus polluting the water with their harmful materials. Other wastes, sealed in containers of porcelain or stainless steel, have been stored deep underground in abandoned mines. But the possibility remains that someday these containers may leak or be found and opened by people who do not understand the danger.

A serious accident in a nuclear power plant could also result in harmful radiation escaping into the environment. For these reasons and others, people worry about atomsplitting as an energy source.

More and more people are asking questions about energy: "How can we avoid the risks that come with nuclear power plants, and the pollution that comes with the burning of fossil fuels?" "How can we get energy without using up all the fossil fuels?" "Aren't there energy sources that don't take long ages to replace—and that are harmless?"

The answer to the last question is yes. In the following pages we will look at some energy sources that are **renewable** and that are also harmless. The "fuel" that is burned to produce these renewable forms of energy will last as long as life on earth, for it is being burned in the immense and fiery heart of the sun.

CHAPTER TWO
THE SUN AS A FURNACE

In many early societies people worshipped the sun as a god. The sun god was thought to be the creator of life on earth. Those ancient peoples did not have the scientific knowledge we have today, but they had grasped a great truth. Without the sun's rays there could be no life on earth. Our earth would be a cold, dead ball of rock.

The sun itself is an immense fiery ball of gas. It is more than a million times as large as the earth but is made of the same elements. The sun is hotter than one can imagine. Scientists say the temperature at its center is many millions of degrees.

At very high temperatures, rocks melt to liquid. At still higher temperatures, the liquid thins to gas. That is why the sun is a ball of glowing gas rather than a ball of rock.

In the heart of the sun, particles are not only very, very hot, they are also pressed together very, very tightly. This tremendous heat and pressure combine to cause particles of very light elements, such as hydrogen, which usually float freely, to join or fuse. In this **fusion** process, new atoms are formed and energy is released.

Someday people will be able to duplicate the process of fusion on earth. The only fuel needed will be a special kind of hydrogen found in water. The immense heat and pressure needed to make the hydrogen atoms fuse will be

An experimental fusion reactor, which may
someday provide us with nearly limitless amounts
of energy from fuels found in seawater.

supplied by extremely concentrated rays of light known as laser beams. The fusion furnace itself will probably have to have inner walls of magnetic force, since the temperatures needed to bring about fusion would melt a furnace made of any solid material known on earth.

Fusion has been achieved in a laboratory, but only for a split second. It is likely that it will be a good many years before the process will be able to supply us with the vast amounts of energy we need. In the meantime, though, there are ways we can use the fusion taking place in the sun to solve some of our energy problems.

Fusion energy from the sun travels out in the form of rays. These rays travel in wave patterns, curved like the ripples on a pool. Some of the waves are very, very short, too short for us to picture. Others are very, very long. Both the long and the short waves are invisible. Only in the middle range is there a very small span of rays the human eye can see. The longer rays within this visible range we see as the color red. The shorter rays we see as violet. In between are all the rest of the colors of the rainbow.

Daylight comes from the sun's rays. Moonlight, too, is sunlight reflected, or bounced off, the surface of the moon. Many of the rays of the sun that we cannot see as light we feel as heat. It is these rays that keep the plants, people, and animals on earth alive.

The sun's rays travel out into space in all directions. Only a very, very small portion of them fall onto earth. Still, the amount that falls on North America alone in one year contains more energy than a trillion tons of coal and a thousand times as much energy as the people of Canada and the United States together use in a year.

This sounds as if the sun should be able to provide

enough renewable energy to do all the work on earth. And perhaps someday it will—directly or indirectly.

The most direct way to put the sun's energy—**solar energy**—to work for humankind is through **solar cells**. These cells are made of extremely small bits of special elements such as silicon and germanium, and they can convert sunlight directly into electricity. One cell by itself is not very powerful. But many tens of thousands of solar cells working together can do a great deal.

Up to the present, small panels of solar cells have been used to power flashlights, electric shavers, radios, small boats, and lighthouses. Larger panels that look like the long blades of a fan have been built onto some spacecraft. Each panel is covered with many thousands of tiny solar cells, all made by hand and thus very costly. But panels of machine-made cells are becoming available.

Now teams of experts are preparing to start work on a huge energy-station satellite, which will be powered by solar cells. This satellite will circle the earth 22,000 miles (35,200 km) away, at the same rate at which the earth spins on its axis. This means that it will always be above the same spot on earth. It will send its electricity to earth in the form of very short waves called **microwaves**. Back on earth these waves will be picked up by huge fields of antennas, fields several miles square. There the waves will be con-

Above: solar power cells. Below: a solar-cell powered cart, which can travel 11 miles (17.7 km) an hour for 6 miles (9.6 km) on just one sunny day's charge.

An artist's conception of a part of the solar
power satellite to be assembled in space.

verted back into electricity and sent out through regular transmission wires.

Building this first power-station satellite will take several years and will cost tens of billions of dollars. After all the pieces have been constructed, a team of 400 astronaut-builders will be sent up to assemble the satellite in space. The plan is for this 100,000-ton (90,000-m.t.) satellite to have wings covered with 34 square miles (75 sq km) of solar cells!

Once the satellite is in orbit, it will be beyond the reach of interfering weather, good or bad. Since it will also be beyond the shadow of the earth, it will receive sunlight night and day. It will need no fuel and very little attention. And the electricity the satellite will produce should not cost much more than electricity from nuclear power plants.

Long before any solar-power satellite is launched into orbit, however, solar cells may be doing much more work on earth. Banks or panels of solar cells are being tried out for use in power plants on earth, to replace fossil fuels. Solar-cell collectors in panels can also be installed on many home rooftops. A panel about 20 by 40 feet (6 by 12 m) can supply a home with all the electric power the family needs—for lights, toasters, fans, and other appliances—if there are at least four sunny days a week.

Some areas have more sunny days than that through much of the year. Home-size solar-cell units in these areas will make more electricity than the family will need. The extra power can then be stored in storage batteries, or it can be sent by wire to the city power system.

Sunlight that reaches the earth can also be put to work in other ways. People have known for a very long time that the sun can warm things—or people—until they are burning hot. To put this ability of the sun to work in a useful way, however, a great many rays have to be collected at one spot.

For a long time, people have known how to accomplish this. As far back as 2,000 years ago, some people knew that the sun's rays bounce off of shiny surfaces. They also knew that when a ray shines straight down on a surface, it is reflected straight up. But when a ray strikes a surface at an angle, it is reflected at the same angle in the other direction.

Thus, long before our modern age, people were building special reflectors that had hard, shiny surfaces and were curved so that the rays striking them were all bounced to the same spot. A lot of reflectors all sending their rays to the same spot could burn wood or cook food.

There are many solar cookers on the market today. A good solar cooker has a shiny, concave surface. It is shaped so that the rays are reflected to the center of the bowl. The cooker must be set on a base so that it can be tilted to face the sun. A pan or an oven at its center holds the food to be cooked. Since dark, dull surfaces soak up heat well, the small oven or pan is often coated with a black substance. These solar cookers are not speedy, but they work. And they do not burn any fuel.

More than 200 years ago, people learned how to make solar furnaces in which they could melt metals. They used a device called a **heliostat**. Helios is the Greek word for the sun. A heliostat uses mirrors—lots of them—for reflectors and has a clock to keep the mirrors tilted toward the sun. Iron, copper, lead, and other useful metals could be melted in these solar furnaces.

A giant solar furnace of this type was built not many years ago in the mountains in the south of France. In the middle of a high concrete wall curving toward the sun is a

Solar cookers are becoming a
viable alternate energy source.

The giant solar furnace built in the mountains of southern France. Sixty-three mirrors in the foreground reflect sunlight onto the curved, mirrored surface of the building, which in turn focuses the sun's rays into the opening in the tower at the center. There, enough heat can be collected to melt any material known on earth.

heliostat. The heliostat's mirrors, turned to face the sun, can gather enough rays to heat metal to 6000° Celsius!

In 1901 some men in Arizona found another use for a heliostat. They built one, shaped like an upside-down umbrella, with 1,788 mirrors in it. At the center of the "umbrella" the men placed a big boiler full of water. As the sun's rays would heat the water to steam, pipes would carry the steam to an engine house. There the force of the expanding steam would turn the wheels of a steam engine.

This system worked beautifully as long as the sun was shining. But people wanted to be able to use the sun's energy when the sun was not shining, too. For this, some way of storing the energy had to be found.

At a plant in New Mexico, just a short time later, such a way was found. In a new system developed there, the steam from a solar boiler was used to drive a water pump. The pump was designed so that it could lift water from underground wells to a storage tank standing on stilts. At night, that same water was then allowed to flow down a pipe from the storage tank. The pressure from the falling water would turn an electric generator and produce electricity. So the heat of the sun, shining by day, was able to power some electric lights by night.

Heliostats are still in use today. Several that are being planned or are already under construction will produce electricity in large amounts. In these, mirrors spread across a square mile (2.6 sq km) or more of level ground will be arranged in a checkerboard pattern and tilted to face the sun. At the center of the field will be a giant boiler, placed at the top of a tower. The sun's rays, reflected from the mirrors to the tower, will turn the water to steam. The force of the steam will then push the wheels of **turbines**, whose rotating motion will power electric generators.

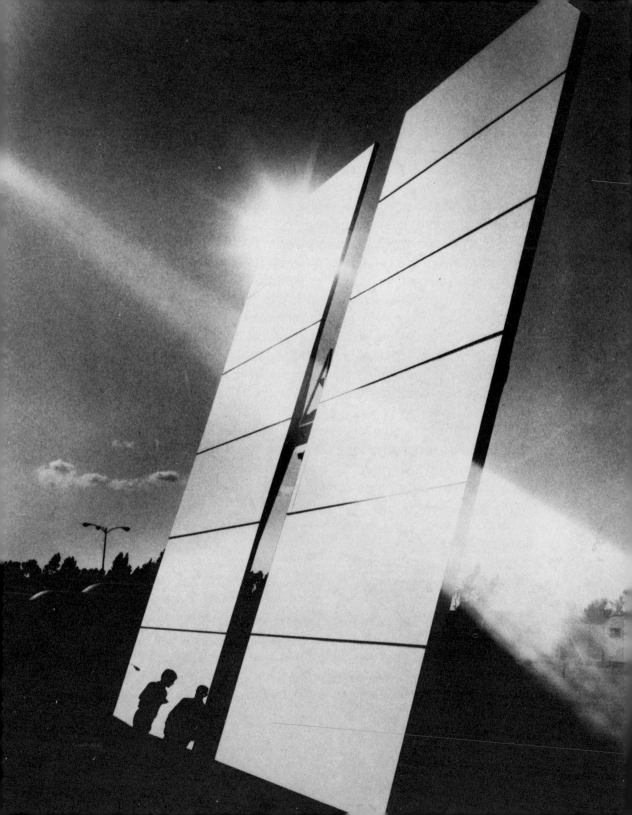

Left: a 400-square-foot (37 sq m) heliostat, similar to the kind that would be used in the facility shown above. Note that in the picture above, all the sunlight is reflected to the steel plate in the "power tower" in the background.

These systems will be very expensive to build, but once built they will operate with no cost for fuel.

Another way to collect the sun's heat is in large, shallow trays. These trays, usually called panels, are lined with black plastic or other material that absorbs and holds solar heat. Coils of pipe lie on top of the black lining or are sunk into it. Glass covers the whole panel.

These heat-collector panels are placed so as to catch as many of the sun's rays as possible. The pipe, or tubing, in the panels is connected to a large water-storage tank. Cold water enters the tubing from the city water pipes and is heated by the sun. The hot water then flows back into the storage tank, where it stays warm for hours.

Heat collector panels, large and small, have many uses. The smallest of them are used to heat water for home or swimming pool use. Larger collectors, generally covering sections of a roof, can heat a house or a school. Many new buildings are being built using these collector panels as part of their original design.

In Florida and parts of the Southwest, where the sun shines most days, solar heat can keep homes comfortable about 95 percent of the time. Even in states such as Colorado and Massachusetts, where winters are cold, the sun's heat can supply about 50 percent of the heating needs of a solar-heated home. A furnace that burns gas, oil, or coal can supply the rest.

In some collector panels, air is heated instead of water. The hot air flows to the storage tank and heats stones there. The hot stones help the air to stay warm, and the warm air can be fanned into rooms as needed.

In hot weather many of these systems can be used for cooling instead of for warmth. This is easiest to accomplish in areas where the nights are cool even when the days are hot. One type of solar house has a huge plastic bag of water on the roof, with a movable cover over it. The cover can be moved aside on chilly days, thus allowing the water to collect the sun's warmth and to warm the rooms below. The cover is then replaced at night to keep the cold out. On hot days the cover is left on, preventing the sun's heat from reaching the water—and the rooms of the house below. The cover is then opened to the cooler air at night. Other solar air-conditioning units use heat-exchange systems that operate much as refrigerators do.

Solar-panel collectors may soon have wider uses. For example, they may provide steam to run electric power plants. Large projects called **solar power farms** are being planned for this purpose.

Here is how a solar farm will work: A large section of desert or other sunny, open land will be covered with rows and rows of flat heat reflectors. Each panel will be tiltable, to catch the maximum number of solar rays. Each panel will have a shiny, mirrorlike surface that will focus the rays on a black-coated collector panel. Tubes attached to these collector panels will be filled with a special oily liquid. As the sun shines, this liquid will become very, very hot—much hotter than boiling water.

The hot liquid will then flow through pipes into a storage tank containing a salty brine. Other pipes will carry water through the storage tank. The water in the pipes will heat up well above the boiling point, and the steam produced as a result will turn electric generators.

Brine can hold heat for many hours. Thus the system will be able to produce electricity at night as well as during the daytime.

Solar power farms such as this one will need a great deal of water. It is planned that the first solar power farm in the United States will be built in a desert area not very far from the Gulf of Mexico. Florida promises to be another good location.

Many of the areas on earth that are very hot and get a great deal of sunshine are also not very far from some sea. So getting a supply of sea water will be no problem. Most of these same lands do not have other kinds of fuel readily available. Thus solar power farms, if they succeed, will prove a great help in easing the energy shortage in these areas.

Solar power farms will be very expensive to build, but the fuel they will use is free and plentiful. There is the problem of how to keep those long rows of reflectors free of dust, so that the sun's rays will not be blocked. But on the other hand, solar power farms will not dirty the air or be dangerous to health. They will not produce waste—useless—heat. And they can also provide an extra benefit: As sea water is turned to steam in the pipes of a solar power farm, the salts that were in the water will be left behind. These salts have to be disposed of, it is true. But as the steam cools down it turns to water again—water that has been desalted and purified and can be used on farms for growing food and other crops.

With all these plans being worked on, it seems likely that by 1990 many homes and other buildings will be solar. Much of their light, heat, and power for machines and appliances will come straight from the sun.

In this chapter we have discussed direct ways of using solar energy. But the sun's rays also work less directly to provide other sources of energy we can use to good advantage. Some of these we shall explore in the following chapters.

CHAPTER THREE
ENERGY FROM PLANTS

An immense amount of energy from the sun falls on the earth every day. Between 70 and 80 percent of these rays are reflected back into space almost immediately. Only a very small proportion of the rest is captured by plants. But that small percentage is extremely important. People and most other animals eat plants grown by solar energy. Meat eaters eat the flesh of animals that ate plants. Thus all available food energy originates in the sun and reaches us through plants.

Plants capture and convert solar energy into forms they can use for growth. They do this by a process known as **photosynthesis**. Photo is the Greek word for light; synthesis is the Greek word for combining.

Photosynthesis takes place only in plant cells that contain colored matter called chlorophyll. Chloro, in Greek, means yellow-green, phyllo means leaf. These cells are the "furnace" for the conversion of solar energy. The "fuel" is sunlight. Raw materials needed for the process are water and carbon dioxide.

Plants that grow on land draw water and nourishing minerals from the soil through their roots. Carbon dioxide, which is present in the air, enters through very small pores in the leaves. These pores are called stomata. Plants that grow in water draw both water and carbon dioxide from the water around them.

The "product" the plant furnace produces is a sugary food that nourishes the plant. Also produced is oxygen, which the plant cannot use and which bubbles off the leaves of the plant somewhat like smoke issuing from a factory smokestack. But whereas smoke pollutes the air, oxygen makes it breathable for people and animals.

What photosynthesis does is to turn solar energy into **chemical energy**. Plants use some of this energy for growth and for forming seeds. They also store a good deal of the energy in their tissues, where it is ready for humans and animals to use.

Eating plants is the oldest and simplest way to use the energy stored in plant tissue. Almost all animals eat some plant food. As the food is digested, the stored chemical energy is made available to muscles, which can convert that energy into **kinetic energy**, the energy of motion. When we eat meat or cheese or drink milk, we are taking in energy from the plants the cow—or other animal—ate. However, only one-tenth of the energy stored in the plant is passed on to us this way. Eating plant food directly makes more efficient use of the energy stored in plants, though plant food does not provide all the same kinds of nourishment.

Burning dry plant material such as wood is another way of using the stored energy. Whenever we burn fossil fuels—coal, oil, and natural gas—we use energy that has been stored for millions of years. The advantage of using wood or other dry plant matter instead of fossil fuels is that trees and smaller plants can be replaced much more quickly than can fossil fuels.

Wood and dried grasses have been used for heating

homes, for cooking food, and for light ever since humans first discovered fire. In many areas these materials are still being used, although in the United States heating homes with wood largely went out of fashion in the nineteenth century, when coal furnaces became common. Then, early in the twentieth century, oil and gas-burning furnaces were developed. These offered clean heat in return for little effort on the part of the householder. They made wood as a fuel seem even more old-fashioned.

Pound for pound (or kilogram for kilogram) fossil fuels provide nearly twice as much heat as most types of wood. In addition, cutting and collecting firewood takes a good deal of labor. This labor has become more and more expensive over the years. Wood is also bulky to transport, and ashes are messy to handle. For these reasons, and because forests and woodlots have been wastefully used up in many areas, wood is no longer one of our basic heating fuels.

With fossil fuels becoming scarce and expensive, though, people are taking a fresh look at wood. In certain areas—such as New England, the Pacific Northwest, and around the Great Lakes—there are still many woodlots and forests. Reforestation programs are helping to renew supplies, too. Whole small towns in timber-rich areas are finding that they can do without shipped-in or piped-in gas and oil. Even some electric generators are being run by burning wood chips. And new types of stoves and room heaters that use wood more efficiently are being developed for home use.

Fireplaces are generally cozy but wasteful, sending more heat up the chimney than into the room. This waste can be reduced. Pipes installed alongside a fireplace can take in cold air close to the floor of the room. Heat from the

Some of our forests may provide an
important future alternate energy source.

fireplace warms the air in the pipes, and the warm air flows out into the room through vents.

Franklin stoves of cast iron combine the cheeriness of an open fire with efficiency of design. Stoves of this type direct all the heat of the fire into the room, not up the chimney. Franklin stoves and improved fireplaces have been available for years, but are being given more attention now.

The grate of the fireplace, the frame on which the fuel is placed, can also be improved. It can be made of U-shaped pipes, for example. Cool air pulled into the open end of the U-pipes close to the floor will be warmed by the fire, then pushed out the upper end of the pipes into the room.

The amount of fossil fuel saved by the use of devices such as these seems small. But if they are used in hundreds of thousands of households, the savings can be significant.

Lumber mills used to burn oil or gas to keep their own machines running. Materials such as bark, twigs, and wood chips were discarded as wastes. Now many mills are burning these materials to power their machines. It has been estimated that if all the wood wastes were burned efficiently, a two-week supply of fossil fuel for the entire country could be saved each year.

Waste materials from trees are not the only plant discards that can be used to supply energy. Not all the parts of food plants are edible. Grain stalks, corn husks, and many vegetable roots, leaves, stems, and seeds can be burned for fuel. Even fruit pits can be used in energy-processing plants.

Immense amounts of garbage—fruit rinds, vegetable peelings, leftover foods, and so on—are thrown away by American families every year. Some of this garbage is

Inedible parts of plants may prove a valuable alternate energy source in the future. Here, alcohol fuels are being made from corn stalks.

ground up beneath kitchen sinks and sent into sewage systems. This may be convenient for the family, but treating sewage is very costly for the community. And sewage disposal systems can cause pollution in our rivers and lakes and even in parts of the oceans.

Many cities collect garbage rather than letting it enter their sewage systems. Some cities pile the garbage and other trash in city dumps or spread it out in special landfills. Others grind, mash, and burn their refuse. Some say that if all the country's refuse were burned as fuel, we could save 10 percent of the fossil fuel used now to produce steam for generating electricity. And in addition the heat given off could warm many buildings. Further, the problem of where to dump the trash would be largely eliminated, since the nonburnable substances left over—metals, mostly—could be compacted into blocks of building material. Such a system is already being used in some cities.

In another kind of system, all the wastes from an apartment complex are gathered in sealed pipes and burned on the premises. The burning provides steam to heat the buildings.

There is also a special method of burning trash, called **pyrolysis**, that has great significance for the future. The trash is burned at very high heat in a chamber with very little oxygen. As it burns, certain gases are produced, among them **methane**—what we usually call natural gas.

Methane is a fuel that can run automobiles or power generators. One government expert estimates that proper use of the methane from wastes could produce 2 to 3 percent of all the energy our nation needs.

Methane can be found wherever plant and animal matter decay. It develops naturally, for example, in farm-

An experimental waste-to-gas facility in Pompano Beach, Florida. The plant can "digest" and convert sewer sludge and organic waste into methane gas.

yard manure piles. About a hundred pounds (45 kg) of manure can produce enough methane to fill an average automobile fuel tank. Large farming enterprises especially could use this method to collect and dispose of their wastes and also produce energy in a way that is both practical and profitable.

Towns and cities can produce methane from sewage, too. First, the sludge in the sewage must be removed from the liquid wastes. This sludge can be "digested" by a special process using large, closed, oxygen-free tanks. The process produces some methane, and in turn the methane can be burned to provide heat to keep the process going.

The liquid remaining after the sludge has been removed can then be spread over a large area and planted with water hyacinth bulbs. Water hyacinths used to be considered only a nuisance. They grow so fast that they often clog waterways. But scientists have found that these plants absorb pesticides and other harmful chemicals from the sewage and leave the water clear enough to be used for irrigation. Later, after the plants are harvested, they can be dried and burned as fuel or digested to provide useful methane gas.

Some cities still spread their refuse on unused land, covering it with a thin layer of soil. As the garbage in a landfill decays, methane gas forms in it. Wells have been drilled into some of these landfills to tap their gas supply. The foul-smelling gas can be purified and then pumped into the city pipeline.

The word "waste" has been used to refer to seemingly useless, worthless, leftover materials. But many so-called waste leftovers are not really worthless. They can provide large amounts of energy to help do the work of the world.

CHAPTER FOUR
ENERGY FROM MOVING AIR

There is a valley on the island of Crete, in the Mediterranean Sea, where dozens of **windmills** can be seen towering against the sky. Each small, garden-size field has its own windmill. The turning arms power pumps that lift underground water to irrigate the plots.

In the Netherlands, windmills can still be seen waving their long arms over the flat land. The force of the wind turns machines inside the mill buildings to grind grain.

Raising water and grinding grain are the two oldest ways in which wind power has been put to use on land. On the water, the force of moving air pushes against cloth sails to move sailboats and sailing ships. This use of the wind is even older.

Windmills to pump water had their greatest day in the United States during the mid-1800s. At that time the central region of the country was being settled. It was an area that included wide stretches of land without rivers usable for water power. But some wind usually blew. As wells were dug on new farms, windmills were built over the wells to operate pumps. The pumps lifted water to tanks. These tanks were able to supply all the farms' water needs.

At about the same period, however, steam engines were also coming into general use. By the late 1800s, most of the ships traveling on the oceans were being propelled

Windmills of the past were used
to grind grain and pump water.
Some are still in working order.

**Windmills may prove most practical for farms,
where they can pump water for irrigation purposes.**

by steam rather than by wind. Steam engines soon almost replaced wind power—and water power—for the running of manufacturing plants, too. Then, in the early 1900s, the spread of electric power lines made windmills seem obsolete even for the pumping of water.

Now, with utility rates rising, wind power is being given serious attention again. Across the United States today more than 150,000 windmills are pumping water for farm use. Thousands of new mills are being produced and sold each year. And not all these new windmills are used to power water pumps. Increasing numbers of them are generating electricity, largely for rural homes.

The possibility of generating electricity from wind power was first put into practice in 1894. It was then that the explorer Fridtjof Nansen set up a windmill in the icy and windy arctic. Wind turned the arms, or vanes as they are generally called. This movement rotated a shaft to which the vanes were attached. The rotation of the shaft spun the rotor—the rotating part—of a generator, which in turn charged an electric **storage battery**. The storage battery, wired to an electric bulb, provided light. This is still the principle behind wind-powered generators today.

Experimental models of wind-powered generators were tried out in many countries in the 1920s and 1930s. Wind power was used on some U.S. farms at that time to generate small supplies of electricity. But in the 1930s power lines began to reach deep into the countryside, bringing to even the most remote farms electricity at the flip of a switch. Farm windmill generators were largely abandoned. However, in the early 1970s, enthusiasm for wind generators revived. By the end of 1976 more than a thousand of them were in use in the United States alone, mainly in rural areas. The number planned for home use is growing rapidly.

Larger-scale projects for supplying electric power to whole towns and cities are also being planned. Government experts feel confident that by the year 2000 wind power will supply at least 3 percent of all the energy used in the United States. Wind-power enthusiasts claim that in the more distant future wind power may be able to supply as much as one-quarter of the nation's electricity.

"But winds are not a steady energy source," some critics point out. This is true. But the air that blankets our earth is always in motion. And even mild breezes, blowing at not much more than 6 miles (9.6 km) per hour, can turn windmill arms and generate some electricity.

To make the best use of shifting air movements, the tops of most windmills are built so that their vanes always face into the wind. Many windmills have a rudder stretching out behind them that acts like the rudder on a boat. It keeps the circling vanes of the windmill turned into the wind.

Sometimes, of course, the wind is strong enough to damage the mill if the arms spin too swiftly. To prevent this, some windmills have cloth sails that can be furled—folded up like the sails on boats or ships—when the wind is too strong.

More modern mills, known as the American type, developed in the 1800s, have vanes that tilt automatically as the speed of the wind changes. In a storm, the wheel turns away from the wind for safety. A mill of this type is called a multivane because it uses so many vanes that they almost fill a circle. The wheel is usually mounted on a tall tower made of steel girders, and at the top a shaft sticks out sideways. The vanes are attached to this shaft like the

**A modern multivane experimental
windmill resembling a bicycle wheel.
This 15-foot (4.5 m) windmill can generate
enough electricity for a rural home or farm.**

spokes on a wheel. Wheels with teeth—gears—turn a vertical shaft running down the tower. More gears at the bottom turn an electric generator or work a water pump.

Many of today's windmills have just a few blades, like an airplane propeller. Three is generally considered the most efficient number. These blades are usually long and thin, and their tilt can be changed to keep the wheel turning at a constant speed. Some of these mills have been designed by airplane engineers, and they are known as propeller types.

A third kind of windmill is the vertical-axis mill, which has its main shaft pointing upward instead of sideways. The vanes are attached to this vertical shaft at top and bottom. Instead of being long and straight, the vanes are curved. Some are shaped like the blades of an egg beater. Others are S-shaped. Since these vanes can catch the wind whatever its direction, vertical-axis windmills do not need rudders to turn them. However, since one vane is always facing upwind, the speed is lessened. Vertical-axis windmills, or wind turbines as some designers prefer to call them, have not been widely used as yet. But since they can be much lighter and less expensive to build than older styles, they may well become the windmill of the future.

The amount of electricity a wind turbine produces depends on the speed of the wind and the size of the vanes. In many areas where there is open country, there is also usually a mild wind blowing at around 15 miles per hour (24 kmph). A vertical-shaft model with a 15-foot (4.5-m)

Two kinds of modern wind turbines.
Both can be significant for the future of
wind as a real alternate energy source.

[37]

diameter can produce a kilowatt of electricity in a 15-mph (24-kmph) wind. This is enough to light ten 100-watt bulbs. In a 30-mph (48-kmph) wind, the same unit can produce 8 kilowatts.

A windmill in southern New Mexico 100 feet (30 m) tall, produces 200 kilowatts of electricity quite steadily. This is enough power for sixty homes. A Danish windmill built in 1957, with three vanes nearly 45 feet (13.5 m) long, produced 200 kilowatts, or 400,000 kilowatt-hours, per year, for a number of years.

Several of these large-scale wind-power projects were planned or begun during the 1940s and 50s. But wars and cheapness of fossil fuels kept them from being completed. Now, once again, the time seems right for more ambitious wind-power plans.

One designer of huge windmill systems hopes someday to build groups of gigantic platforms on large bodies of water where the wind blows constantly. In shallow water the platforms will rest on the bottom. In deep water they can float. On each platform will be a tower 200 feet (60 m) high. Each tower will hold two giant propellers. About 1,900 of these towers, the designer believes, could supply all of New England with electric power.

The same designer also dreams of providing the Great Plains states with wind-powered electricity. Build a forest of giant windmill towers, he says, one for every 2 square miles (5 sq km) of land on the plains. Make each tower as tall as a seventy-floor skyscraper. Put twenty two-bladed wind turbines on top of each. These turbines could generate electricity, which could then be sent through regular power lines. If the wind died down over part of the area, other towers could fill in. For those rare occasions when the wind died over the entire area, fossil fuels could be kept available.

Another, very different dream design was tried out on a small scale in the 1930s. Here is how it would work if done on a large scale: Circles of railroad track, each about three city blocks in diameter, would be built and flatcars placed on the tracks. On each flatcar would stand a round metal tower ten stories high. An electric motor inside each tower would make the tower rotate. The rotation of the towers would increase the force of the wind against them by 80 times! This force would push the flatcars around the track. The turning of the car wheels would turn a generator to produce electric power. The electricity would then be collected by a third rail in the track.

"The big problems with large-scale generation of electricity by wind power are storage and transportation," critics say. But there are ways to store wind power, and in a form that can be transported to wherever it is needed.

One of the simplest ways to convert wind energy for storage is by attaching a flywheel to the mill. As the windmill turns, the flywheel spins. In fact, a set of gears can make the flywheel spin much faster than the windmill turns. The flywheel stores energy much as a tightly wound watch spring stores energy to run a watch. As the flywheel later "runs down," it releases this energy to do work.

Another way to keep wind power on hand in the form of electricity is through storage batteries. The high-capacity batteries that have been developed are giant versions of the small ones we use in flashlights and portable radios. At least one windmill designer has said that a home with a housetop wind generator could store in high-capacity batteries enough electricity for a whole windless week.

Wind energy can also be used to compress air. When the air is later released, it pushes outward with enough force to turn a generator rotor.

Hydrogen gas is a fuel that can be easily stored and easily transported for use in automobile and other kinds of engines. Perhaps the most exciting possibility for the use of wind energy is in the production of hydrogen gas from plain water, through a process known as **electrolysis**.

Electrolysis separates water molecules (H_2O) into atoms of hydrogen (H) and oxygen (O). An electrical charge passing through water causes the separation, and the hydrogen and oxygen bubble to the surface as gases. These gases can then be compressed and stored for later use. And the electricity for the process can be generated by wind power.

Not all the ideas being worked on for the future use of wind power will prove to be practical. But with all these possibilities, it seems clear that the wind will be more widely used as an energy source in the future than it has been in the past.

Above: a prototype of a car being developed by General Electric and Chrysler Corporation. The car will run on high-power storage batteries, and will be able to travel more than 75 miles (120 km) at 35 miles (56 km) an hour without a battery recharge. Below: hydrogen gas is the fuel propelling this new bus, expected to go into general service in Provo, Utah, very soon.

CHAPTER FIVE

ENERGY FROM FLOWING WATER

The amount of water we have on earth remains constant, no matter how much of it we use. This is true thanks to a circular pattern of reuse called the hydrologic cycle. The word hydrologic comes from the Greek word hydro, which means water, and -ology, which means science. A cycle is a series of events that happens over and over again.

Most of the earth's water supply is in the oceans. But as the sun warms the surface of the oceans, and of lakes and ponds, the water molecules move more and more rapidly and finally evaporate—turn to a thin gas called vapor—and rise into the air. Moisture also evaporates in the same way from the ground, from plants, and from streets and rooftops.

As vapor rises, bits of it become attached to specks of dust and form droplets. Many of these droplets together form a cloud. The wind blows clouds across sea and land. Sooner or later the clouds become so heavy that they cannot hold their moisture any more. The moisture then falls to earth as rain, snow, or hail.

Some of the water that falls onto land evaporates as soon as the sun warms it. The rest tends to run downhill, into streams and rivers. Some sinks into the soil.

Most streams and rivers flow into some lake or sea.

From the surface of these bodies of water, water rises as vapor to form clouds, and falls again as rain. And so the hydrologic cycle continues.

How can this cycle provide energy to do work? In several ways. One important way was discussed earlier: Moisture that soaks into the soil carries nourishment to plant roots. But for many hundreds of years people have also been actively putting to use the energy of water that flows on the surface of the earth.

One device that uses the energy of flowing water is a wheel placed in a stream. The axle at the center of the wheel can be attached to a millstone to grind grain as the wheel turns. Buckets on the blades of other waterwheels carry water to higher channels, where it can be used to irrigate fields.

In today's world there are still some waterwheels from the past, operating as they have for centuries. Some still lift water to irrigate fields, others still help to grind grain. A few run machines in factories. But the energy of flowing water is used today mostly to make electricity.

Electricity generated in plants run by water is called **hydroelectric power**. To build a hydroelectric power plant it is necessary to dam a stream. The dam usually consists of a wall of concrete that holds back a supply of water. That water supply, called a reservoir, is at a higher level than the power plant. Water is allowed to rush down with great force, as it is needed, to turn turbines that generate electricity. Then the water flows away downstream.

Some mountainous countries such as Norway have many swift streams. In these countries most of the electricity can be produced in hydroelectric plants. Only about 10 percent of the electricity used in the United States in 1977

An aerial view of Shasta Dam near Redding, California. The hydroelectric facility there can produce over 440,000 kilowatts of power.

was hydroelectric power. Some people think the United States could and should increase its hydroelectric output.

One way to do so is to build more dams. Most of the major rivers in the United States have one or more dams on them already. More could be built on the same rivers, so that the same water would be used more than once. But some environmentalists oppose the building of more big dams. They point out that the river above a dam widens out as the reservoir fills. Land on both sides of the river is then flooded, often destroying farms, homes, wildlife, and beautiful scenery.

Big dams are expensive to build. In addition, all streams and rivers carry bits of rock and soil, called silt, as they flow downhill. When the flow of a stream is stopped by a dam, the silt piles up behind the dam. Usually, before fifty years have passed, the silt has replaced much of the water in the reservoir, and so the dam has less water energy available.

There are ways to increase hydroelectric production without building big dams. One way is to build small generating plants at many of the 50,000 small dams that already exist in this country. "Small hydro" is the term for this kind of power source.

In the past many dams were built to provide water power for mills that produced cloth, paper, or other goods. Then, when energy from coal, oil, and gas became cheap and easy to use, these dams and their water power were abandoned. Now some power companies are building hydroelectric plants at small dam sites. Homeowners who have streams on their property are building small dams with waterwheels attached to generators. The generators supply electricity for all or part of the household's needs.

The most efficient way to run a hydroelectric plant, large or small, is to have it working continuously, around the clock. Electricity must be put to use as soon as it is produced, though, and the demand for power in towns and cities is not steady around the clock. Thus, engineers are looking for ways to use the electricity produced during these "off" hours.

One way is to use the electricity for electrolysis. This is the process described earlier, that separates water into hydrogen and oxygen. These gases can be compressed and stored for future use.

Another way to use this extra electricity is to run electric pumps at a hydroelectric plant. The pumps can lift water that has run through the hydropower plant back up to the reservoir. That same water can then be used over again, without building more dams.

Techniques such as these can increase the energy productivity of flowing water. Other devices are being developed in the hope of generating electricity from the endless motion of water in the oceans.

In some narrow bays and inlets the water sweeps in at high tide to a height of 20, even 40, feet (6 m, 12 m). Some of that water can be captured and kept in containers at high-tide elevation. At low tide it can be released to pour through a power plant and turn turbines.

Another method that needs testing uses waves instead of tides. A reservoir is set up where it can be filled by a number of big waves rolling in successively. The trapped water can then pour down from the reservoir to a power plant below, just as if it came from behind a dam.

Still another method being investigated, called **ocean thermal energy conversion** (OTEC), will use the differences in temperature in the ocean. The water deep down in the

An artist's conception of an electricity-generating ocean thermal power platform that will make use of the sun's energy stored in the oceans.

oceans comes from the earth's polar regions and is thus very cold. At the surface the ocean is warmed by the sun. Pipes can be lowered into the cold ocean depths, while other pipes will draw warm surface water. The warm water can be used to vaporize—boil—ammonia or freon. These liquids turn to gas at much lower temperatures than water. The vapor will expand like water turning to steam, and the expanding vapor can then be used to turn turbines. Cold water from the depths will then cool the vapor once more, turning it back into liquid. This same liquid can then be used over again.

Because the difference in ocean-water temperatures is not very great, not very much energy is produced. And since very large, expensive machinery is required, this process would not seem to be worth the bother except for one fact: Sunlight, whose energy is stored in the ocean water, is limitless and free.

With engineers exploring all these methods, some are almost certain to work out well. The future looks bright for a broader use of energy from flowing water.

CHAPTER SIX
WATER AT WORK UNDERGROUND

One of the most famous sights in Yellowstone Park is the **geyser** named Old Faithful. Every forty to ninety minutes Old Faithful spouts a column, first of boiling water, then of steam, that rises more than 100 feet (30 m) into the air. Geysers such as Old Faithful show us underground water at work.

The huge core of the earth is very hot, so hot that its rock is melted. Where the crust of the earth is thin, some of this heat travels out close to the surface. Wherever a vertical crack in the crust goes deep enough to reach the very hot rock below, and the crack fills with water, a geyser may spout.

What happens is that pressure building from above causes the water to move toward the bottom of the crack. The heat of the rock there causes the water to boil. As the water boils, it bubbles and forces the water above it up and out through the hole at the top. The steam from the boiling water follows. Then the geyser quiets down again, until the water pressure builds up once more, and so on.

The buildup of water in such cracks comes from the slow movement of underground water (called "groundwater") through loosely packed rock. The layers of rock through which underground water moves are called **aquifers**. In Latin aqua means water and fer means to carry.

The water in an aquifer sometimes is under a good deal of pressure and has become very hot from the earth's internal heat. Where a crack in the earth's surface leads from the aquifer to the surface, this pressure can push the water up. The water then comes out as a hot spring.

Geysers are one form of hot spring. Bubbling mud pots are another. Steaming hot pools are a third. Because underground waters carry many salts and minerals to the surface with them, hot springs have been valued for many hundreds of years. People drink the waters or bathe in the pools as a treatment for some diseases.

In modern times hot springs and very hot aquifers have been put to wider use. The steam they spout can run generators or heat buildings just as well as steam produced in a water boiler. And the only "fuel" used is the fiery hot rock of the earth's core.

In Iceland, for example, the earth's crust is thin and cracked at many points. Molten—melted—rock flows up through some of these cracks to form volcanoes. Boiling hot water and steam rise at many other points. Thus the buildings in Iceland's capital city can be heated by steam from underground. Fruits and vegetables thrive there in hothouses warmed by this natural steam.

There are many other areas in the world where hot water and steam come close to the earth's surface. Most of these are along the edges of the earth's plates, where the crust is most likely to crack. In these places the earth's heat can be used to run electric generating plants. Mexico, New Zealand, Italy, Japan, and the Soviet Union have already set up such plants. The United States has them too, in northern California. Others are planned. These plants generate what is called **geothermal energy**. Geo- is from Greek and means the earth; thermal comes from a Greek word for heat.

The main problem in using geothermal energy concerns the salts and minerals the underground waters contain. As the steam is being used, it cools and condenses again to water. This water is salt-free. But only part of the underground water that pushes to the surface turns to steam. The rest still contains all its salts and minerals. This salty water cannot be poured onto the ground, where it would ruin the soil, or into fresh waters such as lakes or rivers.

Engineers are now experimenting with ways of returning the salty water underground. It is important to do this, because if too much water is pumped out and underground reservoirs are left half-empty, the land above may sink. This has happened in many places already—Houston, Texas, and Mexico City for example. In addition, the water returned underground will help to drive more hot water toward the wells of the geothermal station.

In some locations there is no underground water available and there are no natural vents leading deep into hot rock. But geothermal reservoirs can be created. Two very deep wells must be drilled, reaching down into the hot, dry rock below. These wells must be placed no more than 250 feet (75 m) apart, and the rock between them has to be broken up so that water forced into one well can pass through the hot, dry rock into the other well. Cool water pumped into the first well is heated above the boiling point by the hot rock walls. This water is then pushed through the broken rock to the second well, from which it can be piped to generating plants. Later it can be pumped back into the ground to be reheated.

Some oil drillers, while drilling for oil, have instead struck a supply of extremely hot, almost salt-free water 10,000 to 15,000 feet (3,050 to 4,575 m) underground. This water is under great pressure and has some natural gas mixed with it. A practical way to use this kind of geopressure energy store has not yet been worked out. It is one of the many challenges facing people just beginning their careers in the field of energy.

Anyone who works underground soon learns that layers of sand and rock insulate—retain heat or cold—very well. This is true even in the basement of a house. A way of using the insulating property of underground sand and rock to save fuel has been developed. This method starts with the drilling of heat-storage wells into aquifers.

Electric power plants that use coal, oil, or uranium for fuel all produce steam or other hot gases to turn their turbines. There is always hot water or gas left over. One way to avoid wasting this heat is to design and build power plants that produce both electricity and very hot water—as hot as 175° Celsius.

This production of both electricity and usable hot water is called **cogeneration**. It can more than double the usefulness of fuel. The hot water can be used to warm rooms, provide hot tap water for homes, help grow crops in greenhouses, and so on. It can even be used for heat-exchange systems (such as air-conditioners) to cool the air in summer.

Above: steam pours out of a fissure in the earth's surface near Reno, Nevada. Below: a geothermal steam field in California. Pipes gather the steam to be used for the generation of electricity.

At times, more hot water may be produced than can be used right away. The extra water can be stored in aquifers until it is needed, and may still be hot enough for use even several months later, according to some experts.

Two wells are used in an aquifer storage system. Each is about 1,000 feet (300 m) deep, which is deeper than the usual wells from which we pump water for irrigation and drinking. When hot water is to be stored, cool underground water is pumped up from one well, heated, and then pumped into the second well. Later, when its heat is needed, the hot water can be pumped out of the second well, its heat used, and the water returned to the first well. Because all the water pumped out is always pumped back into the ground nearby, there is no danger of the land above sinking.

Some energy experts believe that through systems such as these we may soon be able to make much greater use of the earth itself as an alternate energy source.

CHAPTER SEVEN
PROSPECTS FOR TOMORROW

Before this century ends, many of us who live on this earth must learn to change our ways. We must learn to heat and cool and light our homes, and to run our factories and machines, using renewable energy sources. This book has shown some of the ways in which such changes can be made.

Many of the systems described are in the experimental stage. Others have not progressed beyond the thinking or planning stage. There is still much work to be done.

Some of the systems described will work best in mountainous areas. Others are being designed especially for hot desert lands. Some will prove more practical for homes in the countryside than for homes in the city.

A number of possibilities now being explored may not prove to be practical at all. But finding ways to use sources of energy that will not run out is important. It is one of the most important challenges in today's world.

If we all take this challenge seriously now, the changes we will have to make in our ways of living can be accomplished smoothly, without any discomfort. But if we drift along, we may someday be forced to accept less comfortable homes, less opportunity to travel, and less food to eat. If this happens because we have failed to take our energy problems seriously, we will have only ourselves to blame.

GLOSSARY OF IMPORTANT TERMS

alternate energy source—A source of energy that does not deplete dwindling stores of fossil fuels.

aquifer—A layer of porous rock—rock with many small openings—through which water can travel.

chemical energy—See **energy.**

cogeneration—The production of electricity and useful heat at the same time.

electrical energy—See **energy.**

electricity—A form of energy; sparks of electricity can be produced by friction; useful currents can be produced by a generator. (See **generator.**)

electrolysis—A process for separating molecules into atoms by passing electricity through the molecules.

energy—That which provides the ability to do work. Energy changes form. It may be **chemical energy,** stored in chemical compounds, such as those in plants; **electrical energy,** in an electric current; **kinetic energy,** the energy of motion; **mechanical energy,** energy at work, as in a machine; **nuclear energy,** released when the nucleus of an atom is split; **potential energy,** energy dependent upon position, as when water is stored behind a dam.

fission—The splitting of an atomic nucleus into two or more parts, accompanied by the release of a very large amount of energy.

fossil fuel—Any trace of a living thing from a past age of earth, found embedded in rock, that can be burned to produce energy—such as coal, oil, or natural gas.

fuel—Anything that can produce energy as it changes form, usually in being burned.

fusion—The joining of atomic nuclei under immense heat and pressure, accompanied by the release of a very large amount of energy.

generator—A machine that changes energy of motion into electrical energy. To generate electricity, coils of wire are rotated within a force field created by magnets.

geothermal energy—The great heat inside the earth and the steam from water heated by it; an energy source.

geyser—A natural hot spring that spurts into the air as underground water is boiled by the earth's heat.

heliostat—An instrument that turns mirrors so that they keep reflecting sunlight in the same direction.

hydroelectric power—Electricity generated by using the energy of flowing or falling water.

kinetic energy—See **energy.**

mechanical energy—See **energy.**

methane—A gas of carbon and hydrogen atoms, that burns well and has no odor or color.

microwaves—Electromagnetic rays with wavelengths between a millimeter and a meter long.

nuclear energy—See **energy.**

ocean thermal energy conversion—A system for using differences in ocean-water temperatures to do work.

photosynthesis—The process by which certain plant cells change solar energy into chemical energy and elements from water and air into usable food.

pyrolysis—A process for changing chemical form by fire, used in obtaining energy from trash and garbage. *Pyro* is from the Greek word for fire; *lysis* means to dissolve.

renewable energy source—An energy source, such as water or wind, that is constantly renewed by the sun's rays, by heat from within the earth, or by gravitational forces (as in tides).

solar cell—A device that changes sunlight directly into electricity.

solar energy—Energy from the sun, including light and heat. Also called *radiant energy.*

solar power farm—A very large arrangement of solar collectors that focuses rays of sunshine on boilers to make steam to generate electricity.

storage battery—A group of cells in which chemical energy can be changed into electrical energy, and vice versa. The cells are arranged in a container so that they can act as a unit.

turbine—A machine with buckets or paddles arranged about a wheel. The wheel is turned by moving water or steam.

windmill—A mill that runs when wind energy causes its blades or vanes to rotate.

INDEX

ABOUT
THE AUTHOR

JANE WERNER WATSON
is a free-lance writer
who has written over
200 books for children,
including many
science Golden Books
(Western Publishing).

Mrs. Watson now
makes her home in
Santa Barbara, California,
and has recently
authored for Watts
Conservation of Energy,
a First Book.

Copy 1

j333.7 Watson, Jane Werner
WAT
        Alternate energy
            sources
                        $6.45

DATE			